Conquer Conflict
The Art of Harmonious Resolution

Gabriel D. Simpson

Table of Contents

1. Introduction 2
2. The Anatomy of Conflict 3
    2.1. Early Warning Signs of Conflict 3
    2.2. Types of Conflict 4
    2.3. Components of Conflict 4
    2.4. Phases of Conflict 5
3. Understanding Different Conflict Styles 7
    3.1. The Competing Style 7
    3.2. The Collaborating Style 7
    3.3. The Compromising Style 8
    3.4. The Avoiding Style 9
    3.5. The Accommodating Style 9
4. Active Listening: The Foundation of Resolution 11
    4.1. The Underpinnings of Active Listening 11
    4.2. Essential Skills for Active Listening 12
    4.3. Active Listening in Practice 12
    4.4. Active Listening as a Pathway to Conflict Resolution 13
5. Effective Communication: Beyond Words 15
    5.1. Paralinguistic Cues: Giving Voice to Feelings 15
    5.2. Body language: Hidden Messages in Our Movements 16
    5.3. Active Listening: Intently Absorbing Their World 16
    5.4. Empathy: Stepping into Their Shoes 17
    5.5. Clarity: Plain Language, Profound Understanding 17
6. Emotion in Conflict: Fear, Anger, and Resolution 19
    6.1. Emotions and Their Role in Conflict 19
    6.2. Understanding Fear in Conflict 20
    6.3. Understanding Anger in Conflict 20
    6.4. Balancing Fear and Anger for Resolution 21

7. Negotiation Tactics: From Contentious to Collaborative 23
   7.1. The Role of Emotional Intelligence in Negotiation 23
   7.2. Active Listening as a Negotiation Strategy 24
   7.3. The Art and Tact of Persuasion 24
   7.4. The Centrality of Empathy in Negotiation 25
8. Mediation 101: A Guided Path to Resolution 27
   8.1. Understanding Mediation 27
   8.2. The Mediation Process 27
   8.3. Key Skills for Effective Mediation 29
   8.4. The Potential of Mediation 29
9. The Power of Forgiveness in Conflict Resolution 31
   9.1. The Role of Forgiveness in Conflict Resolution 31
   9.2. Understanding the Process of Forgiveness 32
   9.3. The Emotional Impact on Individuals 33
   9.4. The Social Impact of Forgiveness 33
   9.5. The Praxis of Forgiveness: Implementing Forgiveness in Conflict Resolution 34
10. Maintaining Relationships Post-Conflict 36
    10.1. Conserving the Essence of the Relationship 36
    10.2. Developing Empathy 36
    10.3. Communication: The Key Factor 37
    10.4. Apologizing: A Powerful Tool 37
    10.5. Fostering Resilience in Relationships 37
    10.6. Conflict as Growth: Utilizing Conflict Positively 38
    10.7. Future Conflict Prevention 38
11. Building a Future of Harmony: Conflict Prevention Strategies 39
    11.1. Creating a Culture of Open Dialogue 39
    11.2. Emphasizing Shared Values and Common Goals 40
    11.3. Regularly Practising Emotional Intelligence 40
    11.4. Instituting Fair and Respectful Norms 41

11.5. Encouraging Skills and Knowledge Enhancement 41

Peace is not absence of conflict, it is the ability to handle conflict by peaceful means.

— Ronald Reagan

Chapter 1. Introduction

Conflict. It's an everyday part of our lives that mediates personal relationships, drives world politics, and adds drama to our favorite TV shows. But what if we could take the turbulence of conflict and turn it into symphony of solution, a crescendo of consensus? Welcome to "Conquer Conflict: The Art of Harmonious Resolution." This is no foreboding tome of legal jargon or esoteric psychological theory; rather, we've crafted an inspiring and accessible guide to life's everyday disagreements. Packed with real-life examples, easy-to-follow strategies, and affirming insights, this Special Report will empower you to transform social discord into social accord. As you turn the pages, you'll not only discover the art of finding common ground amidst the most challenging disputes but also enhance your communication skills and personal relationships. So stand up, compose yourself, and be ready to learn and apply the techniques that will orchestrate your path to a symphony of harmonious resolution.

Chapter 2. The Anatomy of Conflict

Conflict is an inherent component of human interaction. It can arise from mismatched expectations, miscommunication, cultural differences, unaddressed emotional debris, or simply from our basic human propensity to have individual perceptions and feelings. However, to delve into the heart of conflict management and resolution, we must first lay the groundwork—understand the fundamental characteristics, types, and mechanisms at play in any conflict scenario. To this effect, we present an enlightening study of 'The Anatomy of Conflict.'

The first step in our journey to understanding conflict is recognizing and acknowledging its existence. Becoming aware of the indications of animosity and discord is central to the process. Often, the signs may be subtle—the rigid silence following a casually expressed opinion, a seemingly innocent tease that leaves a sting, or abrupt escalation into heated argument.

2.1. Early Warning Signs of Conflict

Some common signs of conflict include increased frustration or stress, reduction in open collaboration, lack of mutual respect, continuous blaming and refusal to take responsibility, overtly negative attitudes, and a decline in overall performance or productivity. Observing these signs is crucial as it provides an opportunity to address the issue before it escalates, avoiding significant fallout. The ability to perceive these signs can be developed through mindfulness and active involvement in social interactions.

2.2. Types of Conflict

Once we have identified a conflict situation, it's important to recognize what type of conflict we're dealing with. Conflict can be broadly categorized into four types: Intrapersonal, Interpersonal, Intragroup, and Intergroup.

Intrapersonal conflict arises within an individual. It can stem from cognitive dissonance, conflicting values, or internal struggles tied to personal growth.

Interpersonal conflict, on the other hand, occurs between two or more people. It may arise from miscommunication, differing personality types, or contrasting viewpoints.

Intragroup conflict refers to disputes within a group or team. It could be due to group members' incongruent goals, unequal distribution of resources, or decision-making disagreements.

Intergroup conflict occurs between different groups, often as a result of competition, imbalances in power or value clashes.

Recognizing the nature of conflict enables us to apply appropriate resolution strategies. For instance, understanding an intrapersonal conflict requires introspection and self-awareness, while an interpersonal conflict might require negotiation and communication skills.

2.3. Components of Conflict

Conflict, like any other social phenomena, is composed of essential components. The primary components of conflict include the conflicting parties, the issue or disagreement, the aim or intent, and the context in which the conflict unfolds.

1. **Conflicting parties**: These are the individuals or groups involved

in the conflict. The parties can have contrasting views, expectations, or interests.

2. **Issue or disagreement**: This forms the subject of the conflict. It can be a difference of opinion, a violation of boundaries, or an unfulfilled expectation.
3. **Aim or intent**: This is what the conflicting parties want to achieve through the conflict. It could be an assertion of rights, a change in behavior, or a resolution that caters to their interests.
4. **Context**: This encompasses the environment or circumstances in which the conflict occurs. The context can heavily influence the course of the conflict and its resolution.

Understanding these components enables us to untangle the threads of the conflict, thereby gaining clarity about its essence and potential solutions.

2.4. Phases of Conflict

Conflict does not erupt abruptly; rather, it progresses through distinct phases. They include latent conflict, perceived conflict, felt conflict, manifest conflict, and conflict aftermath.

Latent Conflict: At this stage, the conditions for conflict exist, but the parties involved might not be aware of it. This phase involves potential conflict triggers like differing goals, miscommunication, or resource scarcity.

Perceived Conflict: This stage arises when, despite there not being an explicit disagreement, one or both parties perceive a conflict. This perception may be based on miscommunication, misunderstanding, or lack of clarity.

Felt Conflict: This phase encompasses the emotional reactions associated with conflict, such as anxiety, fear, or confusion. Emotions can significantly shape the trajectory of the conflict.

Manifest Conflict: This phase embodies the overt expression of conflict. Actions like stubbornness, heated arguments, or withdrawal behavior may occur.

Conflict Aftermath: This stage represents the consequences and resolution of the conflict. It might involve an agreement, a compromise, or a broken relationship.

Recognizing these phases facilitates early interventions and appropriate handling of the conflict, thereby preventing it from spiralling out of control.

In conclusion, understanding the anatomy of conflict is the cornerstone to mastering the art of conflict resolution. Recognizing early signs, identifying types, comprehending basic components, and acknowledging the phases of conflict substantially enhance our capacity to manage and resolve disagreements. By grasping these aspects, you arm yourself with the necessary understanding to transform clash and discord into collaborative solutions and strengthened relationships. As we delve deeper into subsequent chapters, we build upon this foundational understanding to cultivate a repertoire of effective conflict resolution skills.

In the next chapter, we examine the various styles individuals employ while dealing with conflict, thereby deepening our understanding of the psychological dynamics at play in conflict situations.

Chapter 3. Understanding Different Conflict Styles

Conflict styles refer to the different ways people approach and manage conflict and strive for resolution. There are five primary conflict resolution styles that individuals tend to utilize, each with its unique way of managing disagreements. These include: competing, collaborating, compromising, avoiding, and accommodating. Understanding these styles can provide a new perspective and tools to transform conflict into opportunities for growth and understanding.

3.1. The Competing Style

The competing style, often considered forceful or aggressive, is characterized by a strong focus on self-interest. People who take this approach are assertive and uncooperative, valuing their needs and desires over those of others. They seek to dominate the discussion, imposing their own solution to the detriment of other ideas.

Competing-style individuals often excel in fast-paced, high-pressure scenarios where quick, decisive action is required. However, this style can also lead to resistance, anger, or animosity from others who feel their voices are unheard and needs unmet.

From a broader perspective, the competing style occurs when one party drives their agenda at the expense of others. Utilizing their power, position, or influence, they push through their preferred solution, often leaving others feeling unheard and marginalized.

3.2. The Collaborating Style

The collaborating style is quite the opposite of competing. It is both assertive and cooperative, representing a win-win approach to conflict. Collaborators work toward innovative solutions that fully satisfy the needs of all parties involved.

People who adopt the collaborating style view conflict as a creative problem-solving opportunity. They invest time and energy in exploring the underlying interests, needs, and concerns behind the dispute, fostering an atmosphere of trust, respect, and shared responsibility.

This style is extremely beneficial in creating harmonious relations, leading to long-term solutions that all parties wholeheartedly endorse. However, it can be time-consuming. It relies heavily on openness to new ideas, excellent communication skills, and the capacity to build trust and mutual respect.

3.3. The Compromising Style

The compromising style, as the name suggests, involves sacrificing some personal goals or values to reach a mutually acceptable solution. Those who favor this style seek a fair compromise where every party gives something up for the sake of resolution.

This style sits at the midpoint of assertiveness and cooperation, neither overly competitive nor overly accommodating. It refers to situations where parties find a mutually acceptable solution that partially satisfies everyone—often summarised by the phrase 'splitting the difference.'

It may not reach an ideal end, but it serves as a quick, intermediate solution when time is short, or when collaborating or competing fails. This way, it ensures that everyone walks away with something, even if it's not exactly what they wanted.

3.4. The Avoiding Style

Avoiding embodies unassertiveness and uncooperativeness. Avoiders shirk confrontation, distancing themselves physically or emotionally from the conflict. They may procrastinate, become unresponsive, or just evade the conversation entirely.

Avoiding can be useful if a conflict is trivial, or if they need time to cool down and think. Sometimes, avoiding prevents unnecessary altercation, or it waits for situations to clarify themselves.

However, the avoiding style can incur certain costs. It often leaves conflicts unresolved, frustrating those looking for resolution and potentially letting minor issues snowball into major crises. For issues requiring immediate action, or those with high emotional intensity, avoiding rarely serves as a sound strategy.

3.5. The Accommodating Style

The accommodating style is high on cooperation but low on assertiveness. Accommodators prioritize the needs and feelings of others, often at the expense of their own. They are known to capitulate, yielding to the demands or requests of others in an attempt to preserve relationships.

This approach can be beneficial if the issue at hand is more important to the other party or if maintaining a positive, smooth relationship is paramount. However, overuse can push accommodators into a position of disadvantage, neglected needs, and suppressed feelings. This style, though conciliatory, potentially breeds resentment or frustration in the long run.

It's essential to note that none of these styles is right or wrong, superior or inferior. The appropriate conflict style depends on the nature and context of the conflict. By understanding these styles, we gain insights into our preferred style and learn to recognize others' styles, increasing empathetic understanding and refining conflict management skills.

In the end, it's about harnessing the full array of conflict styles, becoming adaptable and versatile in one's approach to conflict – the very heart of "Conquer Conflict: The Art of Harmonious Resolution." Understanding different conflict styles can be the key to turn the cacophony of argument into an orchestra of harmonious resolution.

Chapter 4. Active Listening: The Foundation of Resolution

Listening is a fundamental aspect of human communication, central to interpersonal interaction. It's a vital component for resolving conflict, yet one often underestimated or overlooked in favor of eloquence or persuasion. The art of Active Listening takes this core skill and elevates it into a powerful tool for constructively addressing discord. This transformative strategy buttresses the foundation of resolution by cultivating understanding, building empathy, and forging connection across disputed perspectives. As we delve into this chapter's depths, we will thoroughly explore the theory, practice, and utilization of active listening as a means to facilitate harmonious resolution.

4.1. The Underpinnings of Active Listening

Active Listening, a term coined by psychologists Carl Rogers and Richard Farson in the 1950s, extends beyond merely hearing words spoken by others. Instead, it involves an empathetic attunement to the speaker, not just the content conveyed vocally, but also the underlying emotions, intentions, and implicit messages. The listener must be fully present, attentive, responsive, and sensitive to the nuances in the speaker's delivery.

Thus, Active Listening turns passive audibility into an intentional, engaging activity. It's a process that demands full concentration and a genuine desire to comprehend the speaker's feelings and perspectives. By adopting this open stance, listeners foster an environment conducive to open dialogue, encouraging speakers to reveal their perspectives without fear of judgment or counter-argument.

4.2. Essential Skills for Active Listening

To become an effective active listener, one must hone a handful of essential skills. These include:

1. paying complete attention to the speaker, fully present in the moment
2. providing nonverbal cues (nodding, expressions of understanding)
3. offering verbal affirmations (repeating key points, asking relevant questions)
4. postponing judgment and holding one's responses until the speaker finishes
5. summarizing the speaker's words to ensure accurate comprehension

Interplaying these skills fosters a warm communication climate, ensuring the speaker feels appreciated, respected, and understood—an essential step towards conflict resolution.

4.3. Active Listening in Practice

Practicing Active Listening isn't a theoretical endeavor but a practical engagement that requires patience, empathic understanding, and continuous effort. It's leveraged not merely during high-stakes negotiation or mediation but becomes especially advantageous in everyday communication.

At the beginning of a discourse, the active listener establishes an encouraging atmosphere, demonstrating willingness to listen attentively. They maintain open body language, make eye contact, and resist distractions. As the speaker starts sharing their perspective, the listener focuses wholly on the speaker's words, recognizing the embedded attitudes, emotions, and needs.

Throughout this process, the listener uses both verbal and nonverbal skills to affirm their understanding. These could include nodding, paraphrasing, summarizing, and asking clarifying questions. Constant feedback like this assures the speaker that their ideas and feelings are genuinely being understood.

The listener should defer asserting their perspective or offering solutions until the speaker has conveyed their viewpoint. Notably, the listener's role isn't always about solving the problem; sometimes, it's more valuable to simply validate the speaker's experience and emotions.

4.4. Active Listening as a Pathway to Conflict Resolution

In conflict situations, emotions often run high, and misunderstandings are rife. Leveraging Active Listening within such contexts creates an atmosphere of respect and mutual understanding, pulling down the emotional barriers that prevent effective resolutions.

Through careful confrontation and assertive communication, Active Listening addresses the speaker's feelings and perspective without escalating tensions. It not only facilitates the speakers' self-expression but also infers their non-verbal cues, often illuminating hidden concerns or aspirations that might resolve the conflict.

A skilled active listener can transcend beyond personal biases and emotions to comprehend contrasting views genuinely, thus fostering an environment where disagreements can be transformed into productive discussions, and subsequently, effective resolutions.

As we conclude the exploration of Active Listening, it's essential to remember that it's not a solution in itself but the foundation upon which we build understanding and empathy - the cornerstones of conflict resolution. Active Listening does not promise a guarantee of a swift resolution of disputes, but it opens a respectful, empathetic, and constructive pathway towards it. This significant paradigm shift, even if subtly, can make an enormous difference in converting the voice of conflict into the song of harmony.

The journey of mastering Active Listening is not effortlessly traversed - it demands practice and patience, sensitivity and humility. However, the rewards reaped are profound - strengthened personal and professional relationships, and a sophisticated tool-kit for transforming conflict into opportunities for growth, understanding, and unity.

Chapter 5. Effective Communication: Beyond Words

At the heart of every argument, misunderstanding, or disagreement, we so often find a breakdown in communication. To bridge this gap, we need to go beyond mere words and delve into the subtler aspects of effective communication. In this journey, we will explore how paralinguistic cues, body language, active listening, empathy, and clarity can collectively contribute to resolving conflicts and fostering stronger interpersonal bonds.

5.1. Paralinguistic Cues: Giving Voice to Feelings

The old adage, "it's not what you say, but how you say it," may hold more truth than you think. Paralinguistic cues are non-verbal elements that accompany speech, impacting the message's interpretation. They include tone, pitch, volume, speed, and pause.

Tone is the auditory emotion your voice conveys. It can suggest warmth, neutrality, coldness, or any emotion along the spectrum. Adopting an amicable tone even when discussing contentious issues can limit escalations and promote dialogue.

Pitch, volume, and speed can also reveal emotional states. High pitch and volume, coupled with rapid speech, often indicate heightened emotions or urgency, which can exacerbate conflict if not addressed appropriately. Conversely, speaking in lower, softer tones at a moderate pace can breed calm and build rapport.

Lastly, pauses play an essential role, proving the wisdom that "silence is golden." Strategic use of gaps in conversation creates space for reflection and absorption of information, promoting deeper understanding and empathy.

5.2. Body language: Hidden Messages in Our Movements

Body language, technically termed kinesics, are physical behaviors that communicate particular messages. These include facial expressions, posture, eye contact, and gestures.

The face is often the most expressive part of our bodies. The microexpressions that momentarily flit across our features can give away our true feelings, even when our words try to conceal them. Learning to interpret these subliminal signals can greatly enhance communication and conflict resolution efficacy.

Posture and gestures also hold symbolic power. An open posture (uncrossed arms, relaxed stance) signifies approachability and receptiveness, promoting open dialogue. In contrast, crossed arms or closed-off stances can give off defensive or hostile vibes, making communication more challenging.

Eye contact is often seen as a reflection of sincerity and attentiveness. Maintaining appropriate eye contact can thus express your genuine engagement with the other party, contributing to effective communication and conflict resolution.

5.3. Active Listening: Intently Absorbing Their World

Active listening is more than merely hearing words. It involves fully immersing yourself in the speaker's world to understand their emotions, needs, and perspectives. This is achieved by attentive non-verbal cues, encouraging phrases, summarizing, and asking clarifying questions.

Active listening requires undivided attention, signaled by attentive body language: direct eye contact, open posture, and affirmative nods. Encouraging phrases like "I see," "go on," or "uh-huh" can comfort the speaker and add rhythm to the conversation.

Summarizing the speaker's key points, sentiments, or needs acknowledges their feelings and checks for understanding. This, in conjunction, with clarifying questions, ensures effective communication by minimizing assumptions and misunderstandings.

5.4. Empathy: Stepping into Their Shoes

Empathy goes hand in hand with active listening. It refers to the ability to understand and share another person's feelings, effectively stepping into their shoes. This understanding fosters trust, validation, and respect, decreasing conflict risk and enhancing resolution likelihood.

It's not about condoning or uniformly agreeing with others but humanizing them, appreciating their perspectives. Using empathic statements like "It sounds like you feel...", or "I can understand why you might feel this way...", can go a long way in mitigating conflict and promoting harmony.

5.5. Clarity: Plain Language, Profound Understanding

Clarity in communication refers to using simple and precise language to express ideas, requests, and emotions accurately and understandably. By avoiding jargon, bypassing ambiguity, and steering clear of loaded language or offensive terms, it is easier to establish mutual understanding, contributing to conflict resolution.

To achieve accurate communication, it is helpful to express feelings and needs directly. The use of 'I' statements (e.g., "I feel...", or "I need...") can enhance clarity and minimize attributions of blame, making conflicts more manageable and resolution more likely.

This exploration of effective communication methods expands our tools for resolving conflicts beyond mere words. A masterful command of these techniques—paralinguistic cues, body language, active listening, empathy, and clarity—can transform conflict into a harmonious dialogue, bringing us one step closer to a world where discord morphs into accord. The next steps of our journey will delve into the role of emotional intelligence in dispute resolution. As we traverse this exploration, let us remember that every step forward in the art of communication is an advance toward a more peaceful world.

Chapter 6. Emotion in Conflict: Fear, Anger, and Resolution

The voyage into the sea of conflict resolution is riddled with emotional icebergs. Among the largest and most significant of these are fear and anger. Harnessing the chaotic power of these emotions and steering towards resolution rather than resentment is a skill crucial to harmonious coexistence, yet bewilderingly difficult to master.

6.1. Emotions and Their Role in Conflict

Tracing the origins of these powerful emotions can often elucidate their role in conflict resolution. They are not arbitrary or capricious; each emotion carries with it a constellation of physiological changes, thoughts, and potential behaviors that served an essential purpose in our evolutionary past.

Fear, for instance, is a response to a perceived threat. It prepares the body for a flight-or-fight response by increasing heart rate, dilating pupils, and releasing adrenaline. It is a survival mechanism designed to help us react quickly in dangerous situations. However, in a conflict situation, fear usually stems from a different kind of threat: the possibility of emotional harm, such as rejection, humiliation, or loss of esteem.

Anger, on the other hand, usually occurs as a response to provocation. It also prepares the body to defend itself, but unlike fear, it gears us towards fight rather than flight. People often feel anger when they perceive they have been wronged or their boundaries violated. Anger triggers a desire for retaliation, restoration of justice, or reinforcement of personal boundaries.

Plucked from our primal past and dropped into complex social structures and relationships, these emotions may not serve us while negotiating modern conflict. A perceived threat might not really be a danger, and perceived provocation might not warrant an angry response. Overreactions to fear and anger can escalate conflicts, inflicting emotional harm, and damaging relationships.

6.2. Understanding Fear in Conflict

Astute and sensitive acknowledgment of fear in a conflict situation is crucial. Fear can make us more defensive, causing us to snap in anger at the slightest provocation, all in a misguided attempt to protect ourselves from perceived but sometimes misplaced threats.

Challenging fear: Challenging your fears involves taking a realistic look at what you fear, assessing if it is rational or irrational, and subsequently developing coping strategies that can help mitigate your fears and create a more constructive response.

Reframing fear: Fear can feel less overwhelming when we reframe our perspective. Reframing is about challenging initial interpretations or perceptions and proposing a more balanced or positive view. Instead of viewing a disagreement as a threat to your relationship, for instance, you could perceive it as an opportunity for critical dialogue, growth, and strengthening your bond.

6.3. Understanding Anger in Conflict

Anger often flares up when our boundaries are breached. It prompts us to implement changes, making it a potentially constructive force if harnessed appropriately.

Channeling anger for resolution: By exploring the underlying issues causing your anger and channeling it towards finding solutions, you can use anger constructively during conflict resolution. This approach often involves active listening and empathy towards the other party's viewpoint.

Managing anger: Managing anger involves recognizing the early signs of rage, acknowledging them, and choosing a more measured, thoughtful response over explosive reactions. This self-awareness could mean taking a break from the situation, practicing deep breathing techniques, or expressing your feelings in a more balanced manner.

6.4. Balancing Fear and Anger for Resolution

Balancing fear and anger can be a delicate task. The key is to maintain an emotional equilibrium where neither emotion is allowed to run amok and escalate the conflict. One of the most effective strategies to balance fear and anger is through communication, compassion, and compromise.

Practicing emotional awareness: Emotional awareness is the ability to recognize and understand our own emotions and the emotions of the people we're interacting with. It includes identifying the emotions as they occur and understanding their impact. This awareness can lead us to understand the root causes of our negative emotions and manage them more effectively.

Applying compassion and empathy: Compassion and empathy can defuse volatile emotions. When we understand and acknowledge the emotions of others and show them compassion, it helps to deescalate conflict. It makes the other person feel listened to and understood, which can lead to a more peaceful resolution.

Exercising compromise: Compromise can pave the way for conflict resolution. Collaborating on a mutually beneficial solution diminishes the power of fear and anger, shifting the focus from confrontation to cooperation.

Understanding, recognizing, and managing our emotions, especially fear and anger, can transform the landscape of conflict. Viewing these emotions as tools rather than obstacles is the first step toward emotionally intelligent conflict resolution. As we cultivate this skill, we can navigate our way through conflict, not in fragmented dissonance, but in a harmonious symphony of resolution.

Chapter 7. Negotiation Tactics: From Contentious to Collaborative

In the crucible of conflict, the viability of resolution often pivots on the efficacy of negotiation. Indeed, negotiation forms the keystone arch that bridges the chasm between disagreement and resolution, shaping the discourse and guiding the participants toward common ground. This chapter elucidates the tactics necessary to morph contentious negotiations into collaborative dialogues. It encompasses a vast array of strategies, from harnessing emotional intelligence and practicing active listening, to the subtle art of persuasion and the crucial role of empathy in shaping negotiation outcomes.

7.1. The Role of Emotional Intelligence in Negotiation

Before delving further into strategies for effective negotiation, we must first grapple with the meaning and significance of emotional intelligence. Rooted in the realm of psychology, emotional intelligence pertains to the capacity to discern and manage personal feelings and the feelings of others. High emotional intelligence translates into heightened self-awareness, keen social sensitivity, and adaptability in adjusting responses to suit differing emotional dynamics.

In the context of negotiations, emotional intelligence predominantly functions to help us understand the emotional landscape within and around the negotiation process. Recognizing our own emotional state enables us to maintain control, opt for the most constructive responses, and steer clear of destructive, impulsive reactions. Simultaneously, recognizing the emotional state of the other party arms us with strategic foresight to anticipate their responses and fine-tune our persuasive tactics accordingly.

7.2. Active Listening as a Negotiation Strategy

Active listening lies at the heart of meaningful communication and proves a vital strategy in negotiation settings. More than mere hearing, active listening is the deliberate, focused harnessing of attention to understand and respond thoughtfully to the speaker. This practice encourages open dialogue and fosters an atmosphere of mutual respect and cooperation. Instead of rushing to state their points, parties invested in active listening prioritize understanding their counterparts' perspectives, wants, and needs. This nuanced comprehension forms the bedrock of creating effective negotiation solutions, which address shared concerns and shape win-win outcomes.

The process of active listening includes verbal and non-verbal cues such as paraphrasing for clarity, nodding in acknowledgment, and maintaining eye contact. These simple yet potent actions assure the speaker that they're being heard and understood, paving the way for constructive communication and collaborative resolution.

7.3. The Art and Tact of Persuasion

Contentious negotiations often result from the struggle for dominance and the insistent push of personal agendas. To veer negotiations towards a collaborative orientation, it's critical to master the art of persuasion, avoiding aggressive attempts of coercion.

Effective persuasion hinges on building rapport, framing arguments to align with mutual interests, and endorsing empathy over ego. It's about compellingly communicating your position while honoring and understanding the counterparty's viewpoint. This strategic push and pull can successfully nudge both parties toward consensus without the bitterness of zero-sum victories.

Leverage the power of storytelling, data, and positive emotions to make your case more convincingly. Emphasize common ground, shared objectives, and mutual benefits in order to elicit agreement and foster trust. Remember, the aim to persuade shouldn't neglect the other party's needs, instead, it should engage them in co-creating a resolution.

7.4. The Centrality of Empathy in Negotiation

Empathy, the capacity to perceive and share the feelings of others, is an often underestimated yet critical negotiation tactic. It seeds trust, fosters open dialogue, and anchors negotiation in a win-win mindset. A negotiator armed with empathy can shift from combative contestations to solutions-oriented dialogues. They perceive beyond expressed interests, delve into underlying needs, and strive for equitable solutions that inherently respect the interests of both parties.

Empathy doesn't mean surrendering your position but rather comprehending the other's perspective and the rationale behind their stances. When we approach negotiations empathetically, we are more equipped to unravel the concerns deeply entwined in contested interests, and empowered to find solutions that bridge these interests harmoniously.

In conclusion, the journey from contentious to collaborative negotiation demands not only strategic maneuvers but also emotional finesse. Whether it's wielding emotional intelligence, practicing active listening, mastering the art of persuasion, or promoting empathy, the crux lies in shifting from exclusive self-interest to inclusive mutual benefit. Ultimately, turning conflict into a harmonious resolution hinges less on competing to win and more on collaborating to co-create a harmonious outcome that serves and respects all parties involved. As you weave these concepts and tactics into your negotiation repertoire, anticipate the transformative alchemy they can bring: transforming discord into dialogue, contention into consensus, and conflict into collaboration.

Chapter 8. Mediation 101: A Guided Path to Resolution

Understanding what mediation is, why it works, and how to apply it effectively is a venerable skill to bathe in the sunlight of dispute resolution. With humility and precision, we lead you step-by-step down the path of amicable resolution to an otherwise impassable impasse.

8.1. Understanding Mediation

Mediation is a powerful way of resolving disputes that involves a neutral third party, the mediator, whose aim is to facilitate communication between the protagonists. The mediator is not there to provide judgments or solutions, rather to guide the parties in the dispute to a resolution that they can both agree upon.

The mediator's role is defined not by the capacity to reach a conclusion but the ability to shape a conducive environment for conversation. They keep the conversation focused and maintain a civil and respectful tone despite emotionally charged exchanges. The mediator is an alchemy of empathy and tact, using a delicate mix of active listening and effective questioning to unearth the core of the conflict and assist the conflicted parties in finding a mutual resolution. It is essential to note that the power to resolve the conflict ultimately resides with the parties involved.

8.2. The Mediation Process

The mediation process is an intertwined ballet of stages, each offering its unique contribution to the broader symphony of conflict resolution. A skilled mediator dances adeptly between these stages to choreograph the rhythm of resolution.

1. ***Preparation:*** Mediation usually begins with a phase of preparation. This phase allows the mediator to understand the scope of the conflict, the protagonists' perspectives, and the desired outcome. During this stage, the mediator often lays the foundation for the mediation process by establishing the ground rules for communication, like respect, patience, and listening when others speak.

2. ***Problem Identification:*** The next stage is the problem identification. Each party gets an opportunity to describe their view of the conflict, their needs, desires, or the challenge they face. The mediator, with their finely honed listening skills, facilitates these presentations sensitively and impartially, ensuring that each participant feels heard.

3. ***Generation of Options:*** Following the identification of the core issues, the mediator aids the conversation towards the exploration of potential solutions. It could mean brainstorming, suggestion, or even just more focused rumination on the identified problems.

4. ***Negotiation and Resolution:*** This stage is the heart of the mediation process where the actual negotiations and resolution take place. The mediator gently guides the parties to analyze their shared problems from different angles and consider the revealed options. This stage is intensive and demanding, requiring deft negotiation skills.

5. ***Agreement:*** The final stage of mediation is the agreement. Having arrived at an amicable resolution which both parties are willing to commit, the mediator helps them put this resolution into clear, objective, and actionable terms. This part may involve signing formal documents or could simply be a handshake.

8.3. Key Skills for Effective Mediation

Manifesting oneself as an effectual mediator is much more than simply knowing the steps in the process. It necessitates a range of skills and a holistic alignment of mindset and method.

1. *Active Listening:* This skill is crucial to mediation. Active listening involves giving the speaker your full attention, showing empathy, and clarifying understanding through paraphrasing and asking probing questions.
2. *Neutral Facilitation:* A mediator must remain neutral throughout the process. This neutrality assists in establishing trust between the mediator and the disputing parties, encouraging open and candid conversations.
3. *Empathy:* The ability to genuinely understand and identify with the emotional state of another person allows a mediator to foster authentic connections between themselves and the concerned parties.
4. *Problem-Solving:* Skillful problem-solving involves understanding the root cause of a conflict, distinguishing between people's interests and positions, and paving a pathway towards mutually beneficial solutions.

By mastering these skills, integrating them into your unique mediation style, and applying them thoughtfully and consideratively, you become a catalyst for compassion, conversation, and consensus.

8.4. The Potential of Mediation

The true power of mediation lies not only in the resolution of the conflict at hand but also in the change it catalyzes within individuals and their relationships. Besides the obvious outcome of finding a resolution to an immediate dispute, the benefits of mediation are extensive and varied.

Harnessing the process of mediation cultivates understanding and empathy. It offers individuals an opportunity to be heard and validate their emotions and perspectives. It also encourages them to view the conflict from different angles, ultimately fostering a more well-rounded understanding of the dispute.

Mediation empowers people with the tools and the mindset needed to address disagreements proactively and amicably. In embarking on the journey of mediation, individuals not only attain resolution but also gain invaluable life skills such as empathetic listening, effective communication, and flexible problem-solving.

In essence, the art of mediation reaches far beyond the precipice of immediate conflict resolution. It shapes communities, facilitates personal growth, and sows the seeds of harmony in a world so often punctuated by discord. Embracing mediation is much more than embracing a method of dispute resolution, it's about embracing a more harmonious way to engage with our own conflicts and the conflicts of others. This understanding provides us a cornerstone to build a future of harmony, fostering warmth in our personal relationships and radiating peace across the socio-political spectrum. It may be couched in the simplicity of everyday disagreements or resonate in the gravity of international disputes, but wherever mediation finds application, it invariably charts the route towards a symphony of harmonious resolution.

Chapter 9. The Power of Forgiveness in Conflict Resolution

As humans, we are invariably going to engage in conflicts of differing degrees throughout our lives. Hence, it is essential to foster skills like negotiation, effective communication, and active listening. Yet, one often overlooked component in the conflict resolution repertoire is forgiveness. The power of forgiveness, when harnessed correctly, can steer one's path through tumultuous disputes and turbulent emotions towards the realm of peace and resolution.

9.1. The Role of Forgiveness in Conflict Resolution

To counteract staggeringly high feelings of resentment, often wound up in conflict situations, a potent antidote exists—forgiveness. Forgiveness operates in various capacities; it can circumnavigate the vicious cycle of blame and counter blame, reduce anger, and even promote empathy towards the offending individual. In the context of conflict resolution, forgiveness functions as a motivational change, where an individual transitions from seeking revenge or avoiding the offender to a prosocial approach of understanding, empathy, and goodwill.

The role of forgiveness in conflict resolution is paramount. Oftentimes, conflicts lead to a rupture in our emotional well-being through the harboring of grudges and negative feelings which, if unaddressed, can fester and lead to inconclusiveness of conflicts, exacerbating the situation even further. Forgiveness can prevent such adverse outcomes, serving as a bridge, guiding parties from a conflicted state to a harmonious one.

9.2. Understanding the Process of Forgiveness

Forgiveness is not an event; it's a process—a sequence of steps that gradually transforms pain and resentment into acceptance and peace. In the aftermath of a clash, there is typically a commotion of strong negative emotions like anger, hurt, betrayal, or humiliation. Allowing forgiveness to alleviate these feelings needs a willingness to embark upon this transformative journey.

The process of forgiveness usually starts with acknowledgment of the hurt and the role of the offender in the conflict. It doesn't mean forgetting or excusing the wrongdoing; instead, it encourages understanding the conflict from multiple perspectives. This step might stir one's emotional turmoil; however, opening the door to pain forms a path towards healing.

Next comes the decision to forgive. Once you've acknowledged the hurt, you may choose to let go of resentment and forgive the offender. This needs to be an intentional act, a conscious choice made by the person who got hurt.

The third phase involves replacing negative emotions with positive ones like understanding, empathy, and compassion towards the offender. The changes may not occur overnight, but with perpetual active effort, one can gradually transform their feelings.

Finally, the stage of discovery emerges, where the person learns from the experience. This serves as an opportunity to gain insight into oneself and others, providing a stimulus for personal growth and resilience.

9.3. The Emotional Impact on Individuals

Forgiveness has far-reaching emotional implications on individuals entangled in conflicts. By harboring resentment or seeking revenge, individuals remain stuck in the painful past and inhibit their own emotional growth and health. However, by practicing forgiveness, one can yield emotional freedom and get glimpse of a brighter, less burdened future.

Forgiveness helps to reduce negative emotions and amplifies positive ones such as empathy. It allows people to let go of exhausting emotions like bitterness, rage, and resentment. By replacing these harmful emotions with positive ones, people often find a sense of peace and emotional relief.

9.4. The Social Impact of Forgiveness

At its core, forgiveness is an interpersonal process that significantly impacts relationships and social dynamics. When we forgive, we repair ruptures in our relationships caused by conflict. Forgiveness can act as a restorative agent in disrupted relationships, mending the social fabric torn by disputes and grudges.

If adopted in organizational settings, forgiveness promotes positive group dynamics by encouraging empathy and cohesiveness among team members. In familial dynamics too, the power of forgiveness can create a profoundly positive shift in relationships, fostering love and kindness over resentment and bitterness

9.5. The Praxis of Forgiveness: Implementing Forgiveness in Conflict Resolution

However powerful forgiveness may be for conflict resolution, applying it in real-life situations can sometimes prove rather challenging due to its emotionally complex nature. Yet, there are some effective strategies for embedding forgiveness in such situations.

One approach involving offenders is encouraging them to take responsibility for their actions and convey authentic remorse. It opens avenues for victims to consider forgiveness.

As for people who are hurt, they can engage in empathy exercises to see the situation from the offender's perspective. Alternatively, they can seek professional help like counselling or therapy, which can provide them with tools for handling their emotional distress and guide them through the process of forgiveness.

Furthermore, individuals can practice self-forgiveness for their perceived roles in the conflict. By forgiving oneself, individuals can liberate themselves from guilt and self-blame, which could prevent self-loathing and future interpersonal conflicts.

Concluding Thoughts and Further Avenues

In the landscape of conflict resolution, forgiveness is more than just a conciliatory tool—it's a transformative process that impacts individuals socially and emotionally, restoring relationships and fostering personal growth. It's a pathway to freedom from the shackles of hurt and resentment. It's an act of strength that paves the way to a harmonious future.

The allure of forgiveness lies in its concerned approach to take wounded individuals and bring them back into the folds of society - nurtured, healed, and reconciled. Hence, as we steer through the varied paths of everyday conflicts and life-altering disputes, let us not forget the power of forgiveness in conflict resolution - for it is a song on the lips of peace, calling us to a dance of resolution.

Chapter 10. Maintaining Relationships Post-Conflict

Preserving healthy relationships after experiencing conflict is an art as much as it is a science. This chapter elucidates the various measures, mindsets, and methods necessary to safeguard relationships after discord.

10.1. Conserving the Essence of the Relationship

The pivotal first step in maintaining relationships post-conflict is to remember the essence of the relationship. Don't let the conflict overshadow the fundamental reason why the relationship exists in the first place. Conflicts are often temporary, while the power of relationships can span a lifetime. Remembering the shared experiences, mutual interests, and the warmth of camaraderie can do wonders in re-establishing connections post conflict.

10.2. Developing Empathy

Empathy, the ability to understand and share the feelings of others, is a crucial building block for maintaining relationships post conflict. Embrace the mindset of your opponent, live through their perspective, and develop a deeper understanding of their stance. This deeper sensitivity towards their feelings can help in repairing the rifts caused by the conflict. It's not just about 'empathizing', it's also about expressing and communicating this empathy effectively.

10.3. Communication: The Key Factor

Effective communication forms the bridge between understanding and resolution. For this reason, once empathy takes root, the next pillar to erect is that of communication. Acknowledge the validity of the other's feelings and, importantly, express yours in a constructive, non-judgmental manner. Detached, concise, and clear articulation can work wonders to remove post-conflict residual resentment.

10.4. Apologizing: A Powerful Tool

Use asciidoc syntax for listing: . Express regret . Admit responsibility . Make amends . Promise it won't happen again

This four-part apology, derived from the interpersonal communications research of Dr. Gary Chapman, illustrates the healing power of a truly meaningful apology. Expressing regret for your actions, accepting responsibility for your part in the conflict, making efforts to amend the situation, and assuring the non-recurrence of such disagreements, can mend the wounds inflicted during a conflict.

10.5. Fostering Resilience in Relationships

Resilience is an essential quality that can help relationships survive and thrive post-conflict. Providing each other with space to be heard, affirming mutual respect, and ensuring shared intentions for resolution can promote resilience. Regular affirmation of the value and importance of the relationship can reinforce resilience and stability in the relationship.

10.6. Conflict as Growth: Utilizing Conflict Positively

Turning a seemingly negative experience into a positive one is the mark of wisdom. Look at the conflict as a growth opportunity. It is a chance to understand different viewpoints, learn more about yourself and the other person, and find new ways to communicate and relate with each other. Post conflict is the time to think about these aspects and use them to strengthen the bond.

10.7. Future Conflict Prevention

Once the waves of the conflict subside, it is time to establish strategies to prevent future conflicts. Engaging in constructive conversation about what went wrong, how it can be avoided next time, and establishing 'rules of engagement' for future interactions can preemptively quell possible disputes.

Taken together, these strategies illuminate how conflicts, though often challenging and emotionally charged, can provide an unexpected avenue for relationship growth and enlightenment when approached with empathy, communication, respect, and positivity. Dedicating oneself to these principles can revolutionize the way we deal with conflict, fostering not just resolution, but resilience and strength in our relationships. Thus, maintaining relationships post-conflict becomes not just an act of restoration, but a journey of learning, growing, and rebuilding stronger, more resilient relationships. The symphony of harmonious resolution, then, is not just achieved, but passionately conducted, in full knowledge of past discord and future harmonies, bringing out the beautiful symphony that often lies hidden within the cacophony of conflict.

Chapter 11. Building a Future of Harmony: Conflict Prevention Strategies

The inevitable presence of conflict in our daily lives underscores the pertinence of thorough and practical strategies to build a harmonious future. In the realm of human interaction - be it personal relationships, professional environments, or communities at large - the key to managing conflict is in effect, preventing it from escalating into damaging disputes. This entails proactive methods to anticipate potential disagreements, an understanding of the various facets of harmony, and a commitment to purposes larger than the individual.

Admittedly, these strategies might not eliminate conflict altogether, because dissent is a byproduct of our diverse perspectives and unique experiences. However, by implementing these strategies diligently, we can reduce the frequency and intensity of conflicts, and transform them into constructive discussions that foster an environment of mutual respect and understanding.

11.1. Creating a Culture of Open Dialogue

Engendering a culture of open dialogue is an essential starting point. This involves promoting an environment where opinions can be freely expressed without fear of retribution or ridicule. Individuals have to feel safe about bringing forth their ideas or concerns, even if they are conflicting. Transparency and honesty play crucial roles in facilitating dialogue. They eradicate misunderstandings and mistrust, forming the rock bed of any harmonious environment.

In addition to an open sharing of thoughts, a culture of dialogue also imposes a responsibility: the duty to listen attentively and empathetically. Active lecturing, introduced earlier, is an indispensable skill here. By mirroring the emotions behind the words and refraining from instant judgment, we exemplify respect for divergent viewpoints and encourage continued openness.

11.2. Emphasizing Shared Values and Common Goals

Conflict often arises from an exaggerated focus on differences. Hence, it is crucial to identify and highlight shared values and common objectives in any group—be it a family, a community, or an organization. The collective acknowledgement of these shared components fosters unity, mitigates potential misunderstandings and thus, curbs the onset of conflict.

Moreover, aligning individual contributions with overarching goals promotes cooperation rather than competition. Collective success is perceived as a product of collaborative inputs and not a zero-sum game. This shift in perspective naturally deters divisive tendencies, and creates an atmosphere conducive to managing disagreements amicably.

11.3. Regularly Practising Emotional Intelligence

Recognizing and managing one's emotions and the emotions of others—commonly referred to as Emotional Intelligence—is instrumental in conflict prevention. When we better understand our emotional reactions, we can rectify our behaviors and subsequently improve our interactions.

Moreover, by perceiving the emotions behind other's statements, we develop a sense of empathy. This empathy mitigates the rush to judgment that often precedes disagreement, enabling us to respond in a conscientious and respectful manner. Mastering emotional intelligence is thus a proactive step towards harboring a harmonious environment.

11.4. Instituting Fair and Respectful Norms

Developing an equitable set of norms helps maintain harmony by ensuring no one feels marginalized or disrespected. Rules regarding decorum, the sharing of resources, decision-making mechanisms—all hold the potential to minimize disputes arising from perceived unfairness.

However, the enforcement of such norms must be performed carefully to avoid a negative impact on free discourse. Thus, the formulation and reinforcement of these should always include the full participation of those involved. This ensures the compliance and acceptance of the group at large.

11.5. Encouraging Skills and Knowledge Enhancement

Education is a key tool for prevention—it helps individuals improve their skills and enrich their knowledge. The understanding and practice of the prior chapters – from active listening to the power of forgiveness in conflict resolution – when regularly taught and reminded, naturally dissipate potential conflict.

Seminars, workshops, or regular training sessions can function as platforms for such enhancement. These forums need not be overly formal; even casual meetings where such themes are discussed can cultivate a deeper understanding, thereby reducing the propensity to engage in destructive conflicts.

In summation, these conflict prevention strategies involve more than just avoiding disagreements. They are about espousing a mindset that views conflicts as opportunities for dialogue, fostering unity through shared goals, managing emotions intelligently, establishing respectful norms, and continually refining our resolution skills. Remember, building a harmonious future necessitates diligence, patience, and persistence.

www.ingramcontent.com/pod-product-compliance
Lightning Source LLC
Chambersburg PA
CBHW070949220526
45471CB00007B/2954